THROUGH THE LOOKING GLASS

SAMARA PARAKH

The Kindness Foundation is a non-profit and kindness movement that is dedicated to promoting kindness, empathy, and compassion as the pillars of a better world. We run several programs, workshops and events year-round to not only inspire kindness in daily life but also create positive change.

The International Kindness Festival (IKF) is the first of its' kind global celebration of kindness. It is a platform where we share ideas, stories, and experiences that illuminate the path toward a world steeped in kindness.

We strongly believe that it is our youth who are poised to create positive change. The **Book Release event**, a part of the **International Kindness Festival 2023**, is a unique opportunity for our youth to share a piece of their soul through the written word and/or artistic expression, and get their work published. Recognising that being comfortable with your authenticity is a superpower and a form of kindness to self.

ACKNOWLEDGEMENTS

Maya Thiagarajan – Founder, TREE Learning
Diana Shathish – Art Educator & Entrepreneur
Notion Press Publishing

Contents

1. a small introduction   1

2. rosewood   3

3. only a young woman cries tears of black   5

4. persephone's curse   6

5. the edge of my mother's bed   7

6. riddle me this   8

7. disbelief   9

8. the inferiority   11

9. the daughter   12

10. jack of all trades   14

11. dear you,   16

12. everything   18

13. what am i waiting for?   19

14. permanence   21

15. word for word   22

16. the machine   23

17. we call it sanctuary   26

18. i swear off superstition   27

19. the boy king   28

20. woman of the world   29

21. sinful deaths   30

22. interstellar   32

23. the girl who lost everything (even though she lost nothing at all)   33

Contents

24. ocean blues   39

25. what i owe you   40

26. growing pains   42

27. elementary   44

28. the horseman   45

29. pirates in the sky   47

30. deus ex machina   48

31. if the stars gazed at us   49

32. sunrise, sunset   50

33. recipe for potential disaster   51

34. the flying machine   52

35. the golden record   54

36. biomes of life   55

37. the inhumanity of our words   58

38. the long goodbye   60

Acknowledgements   61

a small introduction

though i firmly believe that the words i have collected
here no longer only belong to me
i think it would be nice if you knew where they came
from.
of course, my name and my age are inconsequential to
you, so let's start somewhere else.

i arrange all my books alphabetically
i've never owned a camera that wasn't pink
i've lived in one place my whole life
and i am rubbish at second languages.

one more thing about me is that i have always loved
books.
i have always loved books because i find that they are
quite like people:
an amalgamation of little words and letters that we
have collected over the years
numbered pages, a cover that may be misleading
laced with gems and beauty
but most of all, carrying stories that not everyone may
get to read.
though it may seem trite, part of me has always felt
like i was made for books.

i have always been 'the girl who reads' and i cannot
remember the last time i left the house without one in
my hand or my mind.

what does this say about me?
nothing, but also everything.
for what are the words we make
if they live and die with us?
perhaps it is worth noting that
at least, they lived.

rosewood

knocked on the door but you didn't hear a whisper
of "come in, let's fly away."
the wings of faith have crumbled now
into the rough twine welcome mat on the doorstep.

never has a departure left me so lonely
so lonely
never has a whisper from a saint left me so unholy
unholy

the rosewood has a familiar smell
of times you grew and times you fell
the memory lane has a roadblock now
of nostalgia that you haven't found.

the vines grew up like a sharpened knife
twisted through your brain like the hiss of vice
you thought it was forever but it's ended now
infinite is a lie so finite now

never has a stream pushed me through the folly
the folly
never has a brother ever decked the halls with holly
with holly

the rosewood has a familiar smell
of times you stay and times you stray
memory all so finite now
in lost hazards of rosewood ground.

the creaks of my floors burn your ears
what once was ours are now your crippling fears
the radio silence is so loud
you'd think you'd be over it by now
and you've heard a new whisper
"let's fly back down."
so finite now
the rosewood ground.

only a young woman cries tears of black

only she spends the meagre
hours of her life
filling each crevice, hiding each flaw
packing her perils under layers of colour,
then shimmer, then powder.
she draws the confidence on her face in pencil;
only she knows each freckle, each dimple,
each spot
she sits, remaking herself
knowing there is a 1 in 2 chance this version of herself
will be running down her face when she gets home.

persephone's curse

purest of the purer
they shall cry you a river
they shall forget, they shall starve
and somewhere, shall forget to love.

how his curse would sate her
the fruit of her labour
the mother's care, the mother's call
resounds and wrecks within them all.

do not forget his deeds of yore
demands, tumults within his core
and still he stays, he thinks, he heeds
every year, he loves, he frees.

bring the winter, bring the spring
war between mother and king
bring us your soul, your grace, your health:
you are life and you are death.

the edge of my mother's bed

i used to hang my head off the side of my mother's bed
the blood that rushed to my brain was exhilarating, not
powerful
my head did not touch the ground and my feet did
not reach the pillow
and i did not wish my hair fell to the ground in a
different way.
note: i wrote this while lying on the floor next to my
mother's bed, watching the fan go round after one of
those evenings.
she was reading a book after a long time, and after
i finished, though she did not know i was writing,
she put her book aside, hung her head down over the
bed and kissed my forehead upside-down and told me
about my childhood.
she told me the same three stories she's told me a
thousand times.
i did not mind one bit.
her: (laying on the bed) if you could be
anywhere right now, where would you be?
me: here. you?
her: in my bed.
me: then we are both happy.
(i think, some poetry writes itself.)

riddle me this

"once upon a time,
everything just happened.
the clouds just moved.
objects just fell to the ground.
the stars just blinked and shined and promised and
died.
what was it,
pray tell,
that found the atmosphere, gravity, and the observable
universe?"

"a question."

disbelief

for to live is torment,
and to torment is to kill;

such fickle things defined by pain,
so fickle is our will.

the devoid is treated like a fete:
to fate we leave it be;

to whisk us off to rags or riches;
so rich our rags can be.

this disguise of purpose, yes
misguides our 'kingly' deeds –

oh, the king and all his leagues of men
he never truly leads.

we believe in he that cares as if
he cares what we believe;

we hold dismay so belly-full;
so full of disbelief.

• 10 •

we lost our minds, our wars, our lives
to find our truth; but no –

in plight we cry for anything but
this house we can't call home.

the inferiority

so what if i'd rather study vermeer paintings than
vernier scales?
when i was a kid i could be anything, but not anymore
my stories are just as important as your numbers
for where would be your time machines
your textbooks
your inquiry
if not for the magic of our compelling words
that could bring down a mountain
and of what use would be your computers
with nothing to read
your instruments
if no one could play them?
get out.
you may be a mathematician but you cannot measure
my worth

the daughter

'i am good,' she says.
mother says 'i love you, but you are not.'
'are you even listening to me?' she asks.
father says, 'maybe some other time.'

'i am good,' she pleads.
teacher says, 'not good enough.'
'i am proud,' she whispers.
friends jeer, 'of what?'

'i am good,' she promises.
he interrupts, 'i am better.'
'i really, really love you,' she swears;
'or perhaps i do not.'

'i am good,' she lies.
world says, 'you are right.'
'ha! so i fooled you?'
she pauses.
'you really think so?'

world says 'don't you?
you have come this far
calling for love from those
too scared to give it to you.
you are not just good
you are hope
and here you are, for one more try.'

jack of all trades

i could grasp my chips with a stone-like grip
but they belong to life today
and as death promotes its alter ego
it gambled them all away.

my sugar, my spice, my everything nice
seasoned my salad too much
maybe you can't handle the sweet and the sour
but it makes for a marvellous lunch.

tipping the green-padded tables over
i've thrown all my aces away
i'm not holding my poker face any longer
i'm a jack of all trades today.

my fire will burn down cities
my icy water will douse out
the voices in the wind from the grounded earth
that in me always had doubt.

my life was never yours to gamble
my thoughts are not yours to control
and the sword that cut my slice of life
was forged from the ashes of my soul.

dear you,

do i really hope this letter finds you well?
can i ask how you've been? or is that too forward?
after all, i was always too much.
if you answered me, you would have only one thing to
share
that being the one thing nobody knows better than i
do.

so what is the point?
what is the point of your empty greetings?
all the curses you could never say to my face
and all the curses i wish i could say to yours?
will you ever miss me? even the idea of me?
or have you blurred my face into that of a demon of
your own creation?

maybe i am one, maybe i am not.
but i do know that i am a ghost, forever there, but not
really.
so take it from me;
it was the love that made anything worth haunting.
i know you loved me, in one way or another
will i ever send this?

hopefully it will get lost in the mail.
after all, your true advertisement did.
this letter will become ashes soon, i suppose.

yours,
the shattered fragments of what once was.

receiver's address: everything i thought you could be
sender's address: all the things you promised me i was not

everything

the little fires everywhere
the morning coffee aftertaste
the crinkling leaves
the perished paint on walls
the drawings of eyes
the fingerprints
the dust trapped in the light
the percussion of the song on repeat
the flushes in cheeks
the old thoughts
the long-awaited demise
the bleeds in paper
the broken glass
the loose thread
the chagrin-laced textbook
the weight of the tear
the secret colour
the vanishing flakes
the realisations
the end.

what am i waiting for?

my whole life has felt temporary
as if i'm waiting for something
for some proof that magic is real
and to be swept off my feet for a brand new adventure
every other week.

whenever times get tough,
i have always been able to escape to the closest fantasy
book.
in fact, here is a mantra my mother used to tell me
anytime a friend was not enough:
'a good book will always be your best friend.'

but what do i do when things are too big for an
illusion to handle?
what do i do when i want to run away to a faraway
land but my feet are rooted in the harsh quicksand of
reality?
how many times have i read stories of normal people
being whisked away to fairy-tale worlds
in which they jeer at the ordinary that the rest of us
are stuck in?
where did i really grow up?

well,
i was born in the roots of the faraway tree
i was nurtured by mother goose
i learned how to tie a bowline knot
and five different ways to escape a curse
and all of these are part of who i am just as much as
anything else
and if you would like to file any complaints, consider
this;
what did you think would happen if dragons could
raise me better than people?

hiraeth
/ˈhɪərʌɪθ/
noun
a homesickness for a home to which you cannot return,
a home which maybe never was; the nostalgia, the
yearning, the grief for the lost places of your past.

permanence

it's scary
this big explosion I'm slowly fleeting in
this is all I'll ever know
this keyboard and the fact that my fingers upon it are
the product of every choice I've ever made
and that it affects my life from now
and I can do nothing about it
and these dominos set off that little spark nobody ever
sees
all this sticky stardust in the nebulae everywhere, and
for what?
and I am unable to care enough
enough, so as to not overlook that
maybe nothing matters
but at least it was there.

word for word

"words! mere words! how terrible they were! how clear, and vivid and cruel!"
-oscar wilde

melodious and reverberating, this curse we call words;
manipulating and slithering and cowering and earth-shattering.
sometimes we shoot words like venom and say 'let them hurt';
sometimes they clump awkwardly on the floor and everyone turns to see what fell.

the voice: the means
it chimes like loose change and it rings like a bell and it hangs and it clatters uncomfortably
a cruel tool granted to the wicked and depriving of the meek
masquerading weak words as grand, and hiding strong ones behind the cover of silence;
these sounds that bring tears to our eyes:
that celebrate and destroy and break and shift and lie.
i love them and i hate them and i could not go on without them.

the machine

gleaming plastic smiles
promises and lies
whatever you need, you can trust us.
we know you. you know us.

cogs churn
times tick

make more make more
don't stop don't stop
don't give up don't let us down
one more two more five more

shrill bells
air horns

brick in the wall
cog in the machine
you're important, we hear you.
just make sure you're never seen.

rivers hush
trees thud

big spends big returns
you make only yourself rich
i am watching you
go on, buy.

people scream
people cry

this is for us
this is for all of us
progress, perseverance, perfection
we will last forever.

growth weeps
death's lucrative

produce the money
produce the dopamine
produce the serotonin
just leave the love behind.

artists starve
money lies

exponential detrimental
social physical mental
you are no longer profitable
thank you, goodbye.

we call it sanctuary

they call it a box
four walls and a door,
but i call it love.

where else would i play jenga with the books on my
nightstand?
what else would i cover with bits of paper, and pictures
of things i will not love in three years' time?
who else can glance at her window and spot an old
word pencilled into the wall three years ago out of
sheer boredom?

blueprint, footprint, imprint, sprint
~~noise~~ music, and words exchanged
that find their place here and never leave.
dreams splatter to the wall
hang themselves with a piece of tape
i will ~~never~~ find them again

i swear off superstition

i promise myself that it's a load of rubbish
i won't spend hours in a field searching for four-leafed
clovers
and i'll be damned before i blow a loose eyelash from
my wrist
then i see a red postal van
and suddenly, i'm seven years old again
crossing my fingers and wishing for whatever little
thing would make me feel lucky that day.

the boy king

do not look away
for how does history bear a man
who wears his armour among his own men?
and he who wears the crown upon his head: it tears at
his mind
leaving a barren and bare promise
of the wide eyed child
sworn to be as wild as a forest
and to never sway in the wind
but how can a forest roam
if its own roots hope to rein it in?
heavy hangs the head
that wears the crown.

woman of the world

she was the love in a graveyard;
oh, how she reeked of life.
her gentle hands part all seas
of sorrow and of strife.

i would live for the thrill in her eyes
i would live for the thrill of her lies
i would find the self-portrait in
the divinity of her disguise.

you took matches to the stars in my eyes
you have set them all aflame
you have taught me that the word
'happiness' is more than the absence of pain

hold my heart carefully,
i will tell her.
i don't know if it's all grown up yet.

i don't know if it's for you.

sinful deaths

it appears that i carried too many bodies from their
fake warfront
simple craves against ignorance disguised as an affront
animosity creeping inwards until it devours me
killing more than sword; a signal from gluttony

so you scream and shout until you can see love
wrapped in the veil of guilt after the adrenaline rush
looking at shaking palms, thinking *what have i become*
villainously, the wrath will come

et tu, you brutes? i remember caesar
or so i think as i watch you from afar
but it just seems like there is nothing to be done
is it my sloth stopping me from self-imposing such
fun?

i watch your words flow from that pen with a pang of
jealousy
i watch your exciting endeavours that around me flee

i watch your bond as one i could never imagine
my prevailing envy makes me naught but fragile

the truth is, some loves are just evil
some are to fetch; for my retrieval
but you wouldn't lounge in cool water for me to rust
yet never fulfilling my platonic lust

they say that a want is the root of all damage
disowning while needing is more than i can manage
is it my ignorance that i view as your treason?
unstoppable greed with no good reason

it is but words that would put an end to these sins
yet i let it simmer while my resentment wins
saying this to your face would be a flight-risk kind of
ride
i'll take this secret to my grave along with my pride.

interstellar

are we alone? can you hear us?
is anybody there?
o topography of infinity
don't give us such a scare.

are you real or just a thought?
are you tall or wide or low?
o celestial colossus
is there anything you do not know?

can we bend time and space and weight?
do we fly or do we fall?
perhaps, o city of stardust
there is a universe within us, after all.

a small exercise:
go up to the highest terrace, roof or balcony you can find
where nothing lies between you and the sky.
tilt your head backward, as far as it goes.
does it still feel like you are standing, or does it feel like
you are falling?

the girl who lost everything (even though she lost nothing at all)

once upon a time, there lived a little girl
she wasn't just any little girl, though;
this one, you see, was special.
when she was born, there was a great rejoice
the daughter they had been waiting for
a blank slate, ready to change the world.
haven't you noticed how, when a baby is born,
everyone blesses them to be destined for greatness?
and then they return to their ordinary life
even though they were blessed with so much more
when they were young
what an empty promise, isn't it?
the little girl began to grow, as little girls do
but as for her, well, she was exceptionally fast.
she read voraciously and she spoke like a bolt of
lightning
and her nose was stuck in her books
only, one day, she wouldn't be able to get it out again.
and there was no shortage of praise, oh no;
it was such a pleasant surprise to find such an
exceptional little girl
children never read these days, how lucky you are that
she does!

what a smart little lady!
oh, she's top of her class? i never expected any less.
expected, what a cruel word that is
an identity forced upon you even though you created
it
and even though the only things that can truly be
expected are change, and endings
nobody expected any of that from her, of all people.
the little girl grew and grew, learning and teaching with
every passing moment
devouring her books like they were candy
writing stories at seven and legal documents at twelve
silly little thing, thinking she would carry on growing.
and after years of not having to try to succeed, she
didn't think she would ever have to work so hard.
what happens, then, when perfection is normal?
and when average means failure?
she never stopped reading, though.
she always thought she was like the clever women in
her books and movies
the smartest in the room, the strongest in the room
the one with a beautiful future planned out ahead
and this is a cautionary tale of what happens when you
fall into one too many fictional rabbit holes
because soon, she found that she was stuck in her
fantasy world

she had always held onto the belief that magic was real,
and that she would be the lucky one presented with
the opportunity to wield it

except, the rumours were true.

magic wasn't real.

and if magic wasn't real, then what kind of reality
would she have to become suited to?

all of this culminated into one fateful day

when for the first time in her life

she saw a low grade on her report card

how could she be so stupid?

how could she be good, not excellent?

and that led her onto more such pleasant thoughts

when was the last time she finished a novel in a day?

when was the last time she had to study for longer than
just a day before an exam?

and then it hit her

she was never the only one blessed for greatness as a
baby

look at all these ingénues, all the million others just
like her

she wasn't special at all.

finishing all those enormous books was not some
herculean achievement

it was just something she was supposed to do so that
she could sit aside, happy, after redeeming her singular
good quality

so she was smart
but what else was she?
she didn't know if she was friendly
she certainly wasn't funny
and she was far too serious to be the enjoyable one; she
had to settle for 'occasionally annoying'.
was she kind?
was she ever more than just the one who could read?
and would she be loved still, if she wasn't?
hold on, was she even smart?
or did she fill her head with obscure facts thinking they
would save her life?
or better yet, make it worth living?
if 'average' meant normal, then why was her greatness
treated so nonchalantly?
could she ever get away with being average as long as
she lived?
and why did her love for learning inevitably set
standards that are impossible to achieve?
how could they create someone so fragile, and then tell
her that she is not allowed to break?
and so began the downfall
because every time somebody told her how smart she
was, she felt a pang of guilt
and she was always stuck being the perfect one, the
reliable one, the mature one, even on days when she
didn't feel so grown-up

and suddenly all anybody saw her as was this one thing
she couldn't even trust
but luckily, she realised soon,
(i say 'lucky' because if she had overestimated herself
any further, she may have still thought she was also
worthy of kindness)
she wasn't as strong as she was told
she wasn't as beautiful
and soon it hit her that
she was not nearly as smart
because she could see it unfolding before her eyes
the myriad of those who could outdo her, all of whom
were simply hidden before
she was not any of those clever women she so loved
she wasn't as smart or as cool or as swift
she was just her
she, whose specialty didn't belong to only her
she, who had been loved by all the wrong people
she, who felt like that one piece in a puzzle where it
nearly fits, but the edges are a little too crooked
she, that never fit in, but was truly as ordinary as they
come
she, who had, through some twisted design, become
average
and she, whose illusion of being gifted had begun to
crack

because the one thing that had made her worthy of affection
was the one thing she didn't have anymore.

ocean blues

"now wait," he said; "we should be courteous to these.
and if it were not for the fire that darts
the ground of this region, i should say
that you would be running to greet them."
-dante's divine comedy; inferno: canto xvi

cascaded trenches hidden from view
legs wade about in the forever blue
as if they cannot be snatched into nautical abyss
as if some grand enigma simply cannot exist

seas, loved, but still ignored
shoot for the stars but not the ocean floor
maritime tunes so jovial above
yet waves are such traitors when push comes to shove

an ecosystem snatched tauntingly away
like it was a toy with which she was not to play
so much to live for but not for today
until then, these waves, to stay, to stay.

what i owe you

hear ye, hear ye
lend me your ears

it has come to my attention
that we owe you the words.
we owe you our thoughts, and we owe you that
window
into the heart of humanity.

i will take an oath
we will never run out of rhyme
for as long as words are words
and as long as time is time.

sometimes, it scares me.
sometimes, i look at the words, and wonder:
how can i tie my soul up in a neat little bow
and leave it out for the wolves?

we are all here for something.
the poets are here to detangle.
whether it is the intangible
the frightening
or the truth
we pledge to tear it from our souls
and present it to you on paper, thoughts and graffiti-
covered walls.

growing pains

just this teenage angst
not just young pettiness
that pure rage - unfiltered
raw like the tearing of skin
saltier tears, cry me a river
a tortured soul trapped within
the hushed chambers of regret
weighed down by pounds of guilt
masked behind a promising future
dismissed by a lack of understanding
a kind of alleged lack of responsibility
this endless cycle of capitalistic growth
sometimes salvaged by some dying arts
a revelation of the omnipresent temporary
the horrors of awareness, of consciousness
yearning to get out, clinging to never leaving
instability haunting like a harrowed old ghost
still tempted to fulfil that naïve run-away plan
a cry for some old innocence, a plead for the new
those little skills we thought we had slipping away
is it really happiness, or is it an absence of sadness
passions arriving, dreams fleeting, sorrows sleeping
hiding behind the depths of blank dining-table stares
will we even have enough money for food in eight years

understandable, hormonal, nothing really new to anyone

wishing that this feeling would be unique - not just natural

promising never to unleash this on the child we don't want

again begging that rejected force we once could call our god

who only returns to us allegories, like sunshine and lightning

despair lurking in the monsoons that can never feel the same.

elementary

i just discovered it was my elementary school best
friend's birthday today
i don't think she ever told me her birthday (is my
excuse, because little kids seem to forget to ask such
essential questions)
and when i got coloured ink on my hand and washed
it off with citrus soap, my palm smelled just like a
scratch-n-sniff book i had when i was three
the trace of my never-ending fingerprints grasping the
remnants of a memory
callous exchange and the curse of forgetting
smudge away the carefully lain pieces of a child's heart
slowly but surely, they create a flurry of lost lives.
why do the good times always go by so fast?
because it's elementary, my dear watson:
relativity was a cruel trick played on sentiment.

the horseman

1. conquest

you always hungered for greatness and glory
of course, now the only thing left for you to take is me
the clash of the titans, the fall of the mighty
what we could have made, if we had just let it be

2. famine
the most intrusive of them all, you have stolen little
lives
i have never seen a match for the cruelty in your eyes
i hunger for the day that truth and honour shall arise
but as you starve me to death, you feed them your lies

3. war
some twistingly ironic fight for peace
you claw and teethe and scratch and maim
the gods and men, slaughtered for power
this fight, this tremor, all part of the game.

4. death
merciless slaughter, and so we lie at the end
we would face this one together: we swore
we can only imagine where it goes from here.
you leave me to wonder: is a world built of corpses
worth living for?

pirates in the sky

a dream robbed from its palace in the sky
a pirate stole its thunder
time and hope once glowed, but now it's lost
like the stolen gold and plunder.

a cruel trick on reality
was never captured by
the whole navy's fleet of captain's crew
so it could be left to die.

the plague of words that shoot to kill
will miss their aim, but if one does hit bullseye
your loss can be blamed on the malice of
the pirates in the sky.

deus ex machina

hope wipes the sweat from her forehead
she takes another swing
she disobeys the order
commits treason for the king.

a device, a tool, a weapon
who can truly tell?
was she hand-sculpted by the gods
or procured from the deepest hell?

the remnants can now be salvaged
the futile can now be saved
it was her sudden life
and nonetheless she is depraved.

depraved of sovereignty
of love, of truth, of will
for chance and necessary failure
are the few things she would kill.

if the stars gazed at us

would we teach them what not to do?
would we show them the dangers of getting too close
and how it can create a supernova?
and as we move towards each other
would they yell quietly at us to stop?
we get so close that we explode into a dazzling array of
colours
as they move towards each other
they blind everything around
just to be together
they could ruin everything
yet still, begin something new.

sunrise, sunset

in and out
do we swim or do we drown?
even the dawn breaks and the night falls.

what is love?
knowing and loving anyway.

what is a stupid question?
tell me who i am.

what is your biggest dream?
that i will never have just one.

i can promise few things but this.

sometimes, i just want to cup your heart in my hands;
bruises and all, and say:
it'll be okay.

recipe for potential disaster

1 cup of chocolate
a portion of flour
a spoonful of sugar
some stories to devour
two spices you love
one spice that you hate
a dash of kindness
7 candies (actually, make that 8)

shake, mix and blend until an entirely different colour
is formed.
stir gently
heat until slightly burned, then leave to cool.

serve to all those who know you at kitchen tables,
porch lights and long walks.

the flying machine

oh, you great, grand flying machine!
of splendour and marvels galore!
our grounded feet taken to the skies
with the wind in our hair once more!

come one, come all and have a look!
handcrafted and loved with care
1903, the year we soar
the future's not far – we're already there!

this great, grand canvas belongs to us!
we'll conquer the skies, the clouds and stars
the sky's the limit; the ground's the old
we shall set foot on saturn and mars!

the past, the future, today shall behold
we'll live forever, i say!
we'll live no better than we have
on this fine, sunny day.

oh, you great, grand flying machine!
of splendour and marvels galore!
you make us immortal, forever we'll be
made only to grow and to soar.

the golden record

a world of war, of blood, of hate
we lose our faith, we know our fate.

we leave behind the music, the word
a single promise for no-one to hear.

millions of years of life, of love
of praying to the stars above.

culminate into a small
memoir of the whole, of all.

we teach you how to use it, we hope that you will.
you may not understand, but we will tell you, still.

our last hope: space, please, hold it dear.
we thought. we lived. and i swear we were here.

biomes of life

why do we watch the sands of time slowly slip through
our fingers?
why do we try to grip onto them even if they are to be
lost in the rest of the shore?
thousands dropped, millions forgotten, and a billion
others more.
we'll dream about why it's against the end we fight;
until the waves lap over our souls in the sapphire
seaside tonight.

why do we climb the overgrown saplings and push
through the last branches?
why do we go through it all just to gaze over the leafy
eternity of the jungle?
so much closure in the end of it all.
we'll dream about our innate need to make things
right;
until the dusty light covers our souls within the
forgotten forest tonight.

why are we drawn to the coldness of people?
why do we waste our time caught in a snowstorm when we could build a fire?
from the ice to the snow, to the fires we go.
we'll dream about why we need to freeze to have warmth in our sight;
until the fallen snow buries our souls under the tenacious tundra tonight.

why are we so worried about knowing what lies ahead?
why do we picture freedom as a flat flowery frolic?
we can only close our eyes comfortably under the sun.
we'll dream about why we find comfort in the light;
until the petals scatter over our souls under the dewy daffodils tonight.

we never want to leave the soft, supple sands of sapphire shores;
and we can't jump off the trees we choose to climb in the forgotten forest.
we can't understand warmth without having trampled through the tenacious tundra;
and it's the overcoming of darkness that led us to the promise of the dewy daffodils.

and now the stardust sprinkles our souls with the beauty of the biomes tonight.

the inhumanity of our words

would we be waging wars without words?
without provokers and secrets galore?
without influence that leaves our sadistic human hearts
craving and begging for more?

would our communications make us deluded?
give us the obsession with leaving a mark?
would we dream that our lives will be blazes of glory
when each is nothing more than a spark?

would the hisses in our ears drive us mad?
lead us to perform glorious sins?
would they eat us up as pining doubts from the inside
until our resentment wins?

would we be harbourers of false hope?
be fooled in the blink of an eye?
would we allow ourselves to be changed and
manipulated
by witty words disguised as a lie?

would our history be so important to remember

or so easy to destroy and forget?
with so much care put into a futile skyscraper
when nothing's survived forever yet?

would creative control reign supreme?
would we no longer retain our power?
if the planners took over: drunk on perfection; never
sober
and forgetting our past by the hour?

we can be remade and crumbled with a few simple
words
forget the line between real and the fake
and somehow, the greatest inhumanity lies
in the words we humans make.

the long goodbye

of pits in stomachs, of lumps in throats
the heart i lost, the heart you stole
rusty lockets and dusty drawers
the years are small, the seconds are hours.

i knew each inch, each tear, each scar
you knew my falls, my smiles, my stars
asymptotes and atoms and power and soul
how can a half ever be a whole?

who are we and what is this?
i never hear, you never call
and yet, my biggest fear is
i do not fear this after all.

i will long and i will cry
and i will still find you sometimes
in the roll of a voice, in the back of a car
neither here, nor there; neither close, nor far.

Acknowledgements

It is not very conventional to include acknowledgements within a poetry book, but writing this has been a tributary of a journey in my life and I find that a lot of it is owed to the people around me.

Thank you to all my peers, friends and teachers at school who have nurtured my love for the written word. Namely, my seventh grade English class: thank you for really liking the first poem I ever wrote as part of that assignment. That opened the floodgates to everything I have written since.

I would also like to thank the authors who have always inspired me, because whether they wrote poetry or not, each word they have put on paper has felt like a thousand poems in one: Markus Zusak, J.R.R. Tolkien, Oscar Wilde, Franz Kafka, John Green, Suzanne Collins, Bill Watterson.

A massive thank-you to each and every one of my good friends – you know who you are – for your love and support every single day. I could not and would not be here without you. Especially: thank you to Prakru for being my number-one proof-reader and supporter. I am indebted to you all.

I am so grateful to my family – by blood or not, for your endless love, cheer and support. I write the words for you. Thank you to Maasi and Didi, you are my favourite people to send my work to.

And finally, thank you to my parents, for introducing me to words, music and poetry. Thank you for teaching me to think for myself, and to never yield to those who do not do the same. None of this would ever be possible without both of you.